THE FUTURE WITH AI

How Artificial Intelligence is Changing Human Activities

By

Andres Owen

i

TABLE OF CONTENTS

INTRODUCTION

You may have heard how Artificial Intelligence AI will be the enterprise that will change how you and I will work. You must have also heard about how a lot of companies and industries must do the needful to overcome the various challenges posed by this all-powerful AI with its rapidly evolving technology.

I'm here to take you on a personal journey that will help you understand certain concept and application of this artificial intelligence that many has described as a major player in the new normal that will define the future of our world.

More recently as a researcher, I have concluded that artificial intelligence is already having a huge impact on businesses, more companies are leveraging the AI technology in business operations. More so, as it seems to have a financial cost advantage; while also boosting efficiency, and providing an opportunity for new ideas and markets.

I did come across the fact that Artificial intelligence has enhanced customer services, and increased sales and supply chains, with stronger cyber security; although at the expense of human labor (workers).

While these may be frightening for an average worker in the labor market, companies are using the opportunity to free up their workforce from routine tasks, which has helped not only in productivity but in new product formulation.

I am still trying to understand an aspect of business operation where AI is not needed directly or indirectly. The reason this is attractive is that this imitation of human activities by machines is widely adjudged to favor business owners, whose primary interest is to make a profit in their business.

I and many others are kindly watching, to see how this technology with its inherent challenges will shape the future of mankind.

Three basic facts about AI

While I think that it is still too early to start celebrating artificial intelligence (AI), as holistic technology, I will agree with industry experts on the speed at which it's evolving with the following observations:

1. The sphere of artificial intelligence is shifting tremendously, because of the huge amount being invested in AI research worldwide. Already global business majors are investing heavily in AI-related initiatives.

2. Secondly, there are diverse applications of AI in problem-solving. The effect of the recent pandemic has equally given credence to what AI can do for humanity. From caring for patients, and identifying therapies to vaccine development, there seems to be a kind of an agreement on the important role AI is playing in the effort to overcome the infection. Agreeably, there are huge investments in AI-powered hardware, and related software robotics, which is estimated to even go higher

as organizations and businesses try to build flexibility against future occurrences.

3. If we must benefit from, and maximize the benefit of AI as individuals, companies, and related organizations, we must identify and understand where and how AI works; when and where to use it, and the areas where it is not needed- although, its dynamic cum evolutionary nature queries whether such an area exists that does not require an AI intervention.

I would say here that AI has come to stay. You need to understand how it works, the main types, and its usefulness to humanity.

As you join me in this journey of exposition, in this section I will introduce you to:

4. The key benefits and risks associated with AI.

5. Today and future applications of the AI technology.

6. How you can build a successful AI strategy.

7. The implementation steps for AI tools in organizations.

8. The various technological breakthroughs that are enhancing AI

.A Short Background on Artificial Intelligence
I have read a lot of articles and listened to some empirical analysis on this awesome technological breakthrough that seems to have given hope to what technology will further offer mankind in the future.

I must say that it may not be easy to link AI to a particular era of technological advancement. The reason is that the idea that the human brain can be programmed is at the core of civilization.

Though the earliest reference to AI is recorded in 1956 when the concept of artificial intelligence was first used: in the proposal for an academic conference that was held at Dartmouth College.

Every other record of the history of the AI would either be myths or one of those legendary stories that are told of how certain ancient cultures developed a human-like machine that was said to have emotion and power to reason.

I also read that by the first millennium B.C., theorists from different parts of the world are already building a mechanism for formal reasoning. This earnest search by the likes of theologians, mathematicians, psychologists, engineers, and related scientists may have lasted for over 2000 years before now, with little but notable milestone that can be referenced as a foundation for what is today known as AI.

I still recall what I read about the effort of Alan Turing, the British mathematician and World War II "codebreaker", and the new transformer neural network inventors in providing a foundation for today's AI.

The likes of Aristotle, Muḥammad ibn Mūsā al-Khwārizmī-the Persian mathematician, Ramon Llull-13th-century Spanish theologian, French philosopher, and mathematician: René

Descartes, with Thomas Bayes-the 18th-century clergyman and mathematician, is recorded as those that attempted to describe human thought as symbols.

Although the modern computer is often linked to Charles Babbage and Augusta Ada Byron, Countess of Lovelace who in 1836 invented the first strategy for a programmable mechanism; sometime in the 1940s, John von Neumann the Princeton mathematician, imagined the design for the stored-program computer (the idea that allows computer's program and processed data to be stored safely in the computer's memory.)

But the earliest mathematical model of a neural system that some school of thought has described as the root for current advances in AI technology, is popularized in 1943 by Warren McCulloch. He was said to have coined the term artificial intelligence.

Other notable contributors were Allen Newell, a computer scientist; Herbert A. Simon, a known political scientist and cognitive psychologist; Walter Pitts: computational neuroscientist, in their report titled, "A Logical Calculus of Ideas Immanent in Nervous Activity."

Alan Turing in 1950, with what is today known as the Turing Test, tried to explain the computer's ability to deceive interrogators into accepting as true its responses to their queries. This was before the 1956 Dartmouth conference, put together by the Defense Advanced Research Projects Agency

(DARPA), where the notable AI forerunners in the persons of Oliver Selfridge, Marvin Minsky, and John McCarthy, showcased their Logic Theorists that suggest that a computer program can prove certain mathematical theorems, which was referred to as the pioneer AI program.

It was within the Dartmouth conference that experts anticipated the growth of a thinking machine that can learn and understand just like a human.

Prompting major players, and governments to invest in related research. After about 20 years of basic research promising results were seen, such as the General Problem Solver (GPS) algorithm for instance that was published in the late 1950s.

It is from this foundation that more sophisticated cognitive architectures were developed. AI programming language: Lisp, ELIZA, and early natural language processing (NLP) that chatbots are still using did pave way for what we have today.

It may interest you to know that government and corporations were somewhat discouraged and eventually withdrew support for further research as it appears that an AI system comparable to the human brain seems like a fruitless effort.

It's therefore understandable why the developmental process stagnated between 1974 and 1980. A period referred to as the first AI winter.

There is still no love lost yet as the likes of Edward Feigenbaum's expert systems research sometime in the 1980s, and its subsequent industry adoption generated fresh interest in AI, even though funding support was still an issue.

It was not until the middle of the 1990s that major success was recorded on neural networks, followed by the coming of big data that revived AI.

1

WHAT DO YOU KNOW ABOUT AI AND ITS APPLICATION?

E verything we do in life as humans required some level of intelligence. In my opinion, it does appear as if every one of us was naturally programmed to perform day-to-day tasks based on our level of intelligence.

What then is intelligence, as regards the capacity to execute an assigned task? In my effort to make this concept easier, I will not bother you with definitions as that is not my area of interest. However, intelligence is "the capacity to acquire knowledge and apply it to achieve an outcome; the action taken is related to the particulars of the situation rather than done by rote." According to an online report.

When you configure a machine to do something like this, you're employing the use of artificial intelligence. While there may not be a consensus definition of AI, as observed in a report by the National Science and Technology Council (NSTC), for this book, I will agree with those who define AI as

" a computerized system that exhibits behavior that is commonly thought of as requiring intelligence." And those that see it as "a system capable of rationally solving complex problems or taking appropriate actions to achieve its goals in whatever real-world circumstances it encounters,". As stated in the NSTC report.

Over time, I have seen how problems that were difficult, and sometimes look impossible, become a routine that is easily forgotten. That is the real nature of the artificially intelligent machine. It emphasizes the major cognitive skills such as learning, reasoning, and self-correction

Learning: Ai is designed to receive data and process it as information through rules referred to as algorithms that helps a computer system take a decision on a specific task.

Reasoning: AI can decide the right algorithm, within a group of algorithms, in a given context.

Self-correction: AI is also able to progressively adjust and advance an outcome until the desired goal is achieved.

4 types of AI are worthy of mention.

I will try as much as possible to explain in simple terms the four kinds of AI. Writing on how we should view artificial intelligence David Petersson has already stated how modern artificial intelligence moved from a system that is capable of simple classification and pattern recognition of tasks to a system that is capable of using historical statistics to make forecasts.

It's a result of the successes recorded in **deep learning** (learning from data), that caused the rapid progression of machine intelligence in the 21st century. Today we're talking about self-driving cars, Alexa, Siri, and virtual assistants.

AI that can drive cars, or the one that can win a world champion in a game are still referred to as narrow or weak AI according to an online source.

This is because they are said to possess savant-like skill at certain tasks; hence, lacks the broad intelligence that will make them act like humans. This means that the AI that will function like human intelligence is still in view.

Let us examine the four types of AI as suggested by Petersson and their various characteristics:

Reactive AI. The Algorithms used in this AI are identified as lacking in memory and are reactive. in other words, with a particular input, the output is always the same. It's an early form of AI, and machine learning models that are still using this form of AI are only good for simple arrangement and pattern recognition tasks.

Though it can analyze enormous amounts of data and give relatively intelligent output, it's not capable of evaluating scenarios that involve unsatisfactory information, or the one that requires historical understanding.

Limited memory machines. As the name implies this machine's algorithms are limited in memory, designed to process information the same way that the human brain works and to imitate the way our neurons link. This machine's deep learning will handle complicated classification tasks, and can use historical data to make forecasts. Complex tasks like self-driving can be done by this machine.

Regardless of their somewhat able to do certain things faster and better than humans, limited memory machines are said to be narrow intelligence machines. This is because they're still not as intelligent as humans in other respects of reasoning.

Scientists that have tried severally to make it go beyond this level of performance have said that it requires enormous amounts of training data to perform like humans. They also added that they're exposed to what they described as **outliers** or confrontational examples.

Theory of mind is a future AI that is said to have the capacity to understand human motives and reasoning, as such that could deliver tailored results that are based on an individual's motives; more than the limited memory machines. Widely known as artificial *general intelligence* (AGI), this AI when fully achieved will be able to learn with fewer examples, compared to limited memory machines.

Particularly on contextualizing and generalizing information, and deducing knowledge to established problems. This interestingly makes this AI Artificial emotional intelligence;

having the ability to sense human emotions and understand humans.

While scientists are working toward this, the present systems do not show the theory of mind characteristics; hence, do not exhibit self-awareness which is the next target of AI experts.

Self-aware AI (artificial superintelligence}. This AI seems the main destination of future AI as it is expected to have the ability to be aware of the mental condition of other things, plus self. Hence the term *Self-aware AI, or artificial superintelligence* (ASI). Generally described as a machine that is as intelligent as the human general intelligence, and in principle can surpass the human reasoning through the creation of better intelligent versions of itself.

The downside of this is that while very little is known about the human intelligence itself, how can a machine act as its replica. At this juncture, let me say that Artificial intelligence involves diverse tools that are subject to different technologies.

Summarizing these Types of Artificial Intelligence

The general view of the latest advances in artificial intelligence research is that emotional and intelligent machines are already here with us, as machines now understand verbal commands. It can also distinguish pictures, drive cars, and play games more efficiently than humans. Enthusiasts believed that sooner machines will also walk like us.

Although a recent White House report on artificial intelligence may have taken a skeptical view of this dream, by saying that in the next 20 years, machines are unlikely to "exhibit broadly-applicable intelligence comparable to or exceeding that of humans," it does suggest that in the years to come, "machines will reach and exceed human performance on more and more tasks." It however did not emphasize broadly how those capabilities will develop.

Just like industry experts have suggested, the report seems to have focused more on "mainstream" AI tools mainly machine learning and deep learning. These above-mentioned technologies can defeat humans in very complicated things like games.

These present intelligent systems can undertake large amounts of data and make sophisticated calculations very fast; although they still lack some ability that future AI is hoping to have.

The consensus among Ai scholars is that there's a need to rather than just teach machines to learn, have AI that will overcome the limits that characterized the four types of artificial intelligence. Thus, overcoming the obstacles that differentiate machines from humans.

2

REASONS AI IS NEEDED IN BUSINESS AND ORGANIZATIONS

Just like many, you might be wondering why people keep talking about AI. Those for and those against these wonderful innovations.

Based on findings by IDC that suggest that by 2025, the totality of data produced worldwide will get to 175 zettabytes, stated differently: 175 billion terabytes; indicating a surprisingly 430% rise over the 33 zettabytes of data available as of 2018.

This is very beneficial to establishments that are data-driven in decision-making. This increase in data will help improve their line of business; as the raw material for the new business intelligence and improved business operation.

Arguably, AI is the mainstay of these companies in storing this huge data. In the thinking of Kathleen Walch, the Cognilytica analyst, AI and large data are symbiotic in 21st-century business accomplishments.

This suggests that Deep learning, which is a subgroup of AI and machine learning, develops large data stores to identify the subtle patterns and connections in large data that can give establishments business benefits.

Recall also that AI experts have praised AI's ability to create significant predictions, which requires not just huge stores of data but a high quality of data, to be able to accomplish expected results that are different from mimic human biases. The Cloud computing environments, for instance, have provided successful computational influence desired in managing big data in an accessible and less rigid architecture, for AI applications and also creating bigger access to users.

Impact of AI on innovativeness

Now I will examine the essence of AI in 21st-century business operations. I have read a lot about the strategic role AI is playing in the new economic system of the world. Many have likened this laudable value to that provided by electricity around the early part of the 20th century which saw a rapid transformation of industries. Just as electrifying aided a lot of industries, for instance, the manufacturing sector, and leading also to the establishment of fresh industries like mass communications. AI seems to be strategic in modern-day enterprises because of its scope, scale, dynamism, and complexities in managing the business in a way that humans could not do without it.

In a recent interview Chris Brahm, partner, and director at Bain & Company, agreed to this because AI has impacted positively on business operations and will continue to do so owing to its ability to automate and assist in doing works that humans were known to be doing before now.

The few success recorded with the use of AI is expected to increase and possibly exceed those made by current factory automation tools.

Similarly, its power to capture and analyze vast volumes of data is making it the most efficient way of completing tasks and adjusting easily to workflow patterns.

AI is designed to assist man in all his endeavors. Different fields are applying it to facilitate services. Doctors will need it for medical diagnoses, and call center workers use it in handling customer queries and complaints. We already know how effective Ai is in security, in terms of responding to cyber-security threats, the list is endless

The major concern about Ai is that it is eliminating certain jobs and causing unemployment.

The huge benefits of AI in the enterprise.
Many companies are now employing the use of AI to facilitate already established operations instead of changing the entire model. This has astronomically improved the fortunes of many business enterprises, in terms of productivity and efficiency in service delivery. This is a major benefit that AI offers the business world.

Let me show you the other key benefits of AI in the business world:

Customer service enhanced- This comes from the ability of AI to facilitate more targeted customer service messages. This is evident in a 2019 research study by MIT Sloan Management and Boston Consulting Group, which ranked AI high on this.

Improved monitoring. Its ability to process real-time data ensures that organizations can implement near-instantaneous evaluation; a very good example here would be a factory floor, using image recognition software and machine learning models for quality control procedures and to monitor production and report problems.

Speed up product development. AI provides the opportunity for shorter product development cycles. It also will reduce the time amid design and commercialization which is good for a quicker ROI

More acceptable quality. Since AI tends to reduce errors, organizations expect a better quality of output and compliance to standards on tasks ordinarily done manually by people or done with outdated automation tools.

AI can perfectly do things like extracting transforming and loading information in a way that reduces cost, errors, and time.

Better management of skills- Companies are using business AI software to manage staff hiring and encourage better corporate communications that are devoid of bias in selecting candidates.

We all know how Advances in speech recognition and related NLP tools have given chatbots the ability to give a targeted message in form of responses to job candidates and employees.

Innovation in the Business model- Digital inclined organizations like Amazon and Airbnb, are now using AI to implement new business ideas. Just as every other growth-minded company is trying to find an AI-enabled business model that will transform into more revenue for the company. This opinion has been voiced by Andrew Ng, a pioneer of AI development at Google and Baidu, who is the CEO and co-founder of Landing AI.

Are there risks occasioned by AI?

Worker mistrust. Is among the major risks in the effective use of AI in the business world. This is so because employees seem to be afraid of AI and are often unconvinced of its value in the workstation. Some finding has also given credence to this assertion

An article from the Brookings Institute, titled "Automation and Artificial Intelligence: How Machines Are Affecting People and Places, shows that about 36 million jobs may be affected negatively by automation sooner.

It sighted office administration, production food preparation, and transportation as the worst-hit, or the most venerable.

The study concluded that by 2030, almost all occupations will be affected somehow by AI-enabled automation. Although AI according to Gartner is introducing new job opportunities. It makes it a "net-positive job driver" in the year 2020 with over 500,000 excess jobs than it eliminated. I will say that this is indeed a landmark achievement that makes her the potential to be taped by any organization that wants to grow. And by the year 2025, it's predicted that AI will produce about 2 million real new jobs.

With this lack of worker trust, however, the true targeted benefit of AI will be difficult to be accomplished.

In his view, Beena Ammanath, an AI managing director at Deloitte Consulting LLP, noted recently in a publication that it is the main risk that businesses will fight first before implementing the technology.

In his words, "I've seen cases where the algorithm works perfectly, but the worker isn't trained or motivated to use it," Ammanath observed.

I think the main issue here is that as AI models turn more sophisticated, trying to explain and make workers understand how an AI draws its conclusion becomes even harder, especially for frontline workers that need to trust the AI to make decisions.

Therefore I encourage companies to put users first, just as AI experts have stated in their various opinion.

The logic here, they say is that "data scientists" for instance are expected to focus on providing relevant information to the particular domain professional, instead of trying to know the technique of a model and how it works.

Understandably, a machine learning model that forecasts the risk of a patient being readmitted may often cause the physician to want a clarification of the fundamental medical reasons; the same way a discharge planner would want to identify the likelihood of readmission.

To summarize this and help you understand the biggest risks to be afraid of in the AI technology, all I would say is that:

- **Errors: erroneous** algorithms often lead to AI errors that can be dangerous because of the huge size of transactions that it processes. In their opinion, Bain & Company's Brahm noted that "Humans might make 30 mistakes in a day, but a bot handling millions of transactions a day magnifies any error,".

- **Immoral and unintended practices. AI users must not be involved in** unethical AI. It has been reported of certain racial biases sweltered into the AI-based risk prediction tools that some judges adopted in sentencing criminals and deciding bail.

- There is also the need to be aware of the **unintended**

consequences of using AI in making business verdicts. An organization for instance, that uses AI to determine the pricing based on rivalry from competitors, may charge more in poor neighborhoods where there is less competition, this AI logical approval may not be the strategy the company intends to accomplish.

- **Destruction of main skills.** Though not often considered this risk of AI is also worthy of mention. I still recall an article I read sometime about the two plane crashes between Boeing 737 Max jets. Experts it says expressed concern about the possibility that its pilots were losing basic flying skills, or the ability to use them. This is because the jet depends on collective amounts of AI in the cockpit.

Apart from just being an accident, this observed possibility should make organizations want to consider preserving certain human workforce skills while exploring the full advantage of AI, experts say.

You will find below some major applications of AI in business, and industry-related examples of AI use.

3

CURRENT CREATIVE BUSINESS APPLICATIONS
OF AI

A simple Google search for the newest business applications of AI will show thousands of results, which shows that lots of companies are using Ai in their industry.

This AI application could be something from simple to complex across industries. We simply cannot find an AI replacement in financial services that is said to be an early adopter.

The same is the case with healthcare, education, marketing, and retail-related services.

AI is doing wonders in the commercial department of almost, every industry. In terms of marketing, finance, human resources, IT, and related business operations.

You are already aware of the incorporation of a range of AI applications as natural language generation tools for customer service operation; deep learning platforms applied in automated driving and facial recognition tools for law enforcement.

A very good example of the use of AI in multiple industries and business departments will surface here in form of:

9. AI chatbots

10. AI-powered apps

11. Virtual financial assistance

12. Predictive analytics

13. Dept. collection assistance etc.

Financial-related services. AI is changing how banks function and how customers bank. It is quite interesting how Chase Bank, Bank of America, Wells Fargo, and others are now using AI to expand back-office systems; also, automating customer service, thereby creating new opportunities.

Manufacturing-related services. There are robots, that are now working on assembly lines and in warehouses assisting humans. Some factories use AI to forecast maintenance requirements; just as machine learning algorithms identify purchasing habits and can forecast product demand for effective production planning.

Agriculture-related services. The huge agriculture industry is applying AI to get better and healthier crops, reduce human efforts, and organize data for effective management

.**Legal Services- In case you're not** aware yet, the document-intensive legal arena is dependent on AI to facilitate a lot of things, especially to save time and improve client service. Law firms are adopting machine learning to mine data and forecast outcomes.

A lot of them are also using computer vision to categorize and retrieve information from documents, and NLP for requests information interpretation.

I still recall reading about how Vince DiMascio talks about how his team is using AI and robotic process automation at the big immigration law firm where he is working as the CIO and CTO.

Educational services. You're also aware of the usefulness of AI In automating the boring process of categorizing assessments, Today AI is assessing students and familiarizing curricula with their requirements and more.

Information Technology. IT firms are today adopting natural language processing in automating user requests for their services. They're simply using machine learning in information technology system management (ITSM) data, in other to have a deeper understanding of their infrastructure and procedures.

Insight about Evolution of AI Use

The extent of AI application in organizations is rapidly expanding and new things evolving daily despite the uncertainty that has characterized the commercial world.

While companies continue to grapple with the consequences of the recent pandemic, AI is among the useful things that are helping companies strategize on how to stay afloat, this view is also voiced recently by an AI platform provider, Arijit Sengupta, the CEO of Aible.

It is believed that model creation will become quicker in such a way that will see predictive AI applications models working more for salespeople; as such makes them stakeholders in the creation of real-time empirical data for regular analysis. As a rule, organizations applying AI are advised to always, get end-user feedback regularly because certain issues occur at the output level before the system recognizes it.

If you want to have a detailed insight about AI use cases and how it is evolving, George Lawton's revealing article on the "eight emergings AI use cases in the enterprise." Will be a handy resource.

Some of the major things I find very interesting about this is the "digital twin technology in business" that takes care of hard assets like heavy machinery, with rising investment in AI plus machine learning in supply chain administration.

4

AI EMBRACING IN ORGANIZATIONS

Very Recent studies have suggested that AI deployments in the enterprise are growing at a rapid rate. It is believed that by the end of 2022, for example, the average number of AI schemes per company will rise to about 35 which will be about a 250% increase compared to the 10 schemes that were the case as of 2020.

Some school of thought though is skeptical about this projected growth, but a careful analysis suggested that there was a 10-percentage increase in enterprise AI acceptance from 4% to 14% in 2019.

Statistics by Morning Consult on behalf of IBM indicate IBM's "Global AI Adoption Index 2021," while AI acceptance was almost flat within 2020 and 2021, noteworthy investments are scheduled. It indicated that "Nearly three-quarters of companies are now using AI (31%) or exploring its use (43%)." Some experts that spoke about this data-changing business needs amidst the recent pandemic believed that the pandemic is a propelling factor in the rapid Ai adoption.

The record further shows that 43% of the companies agreed that their businesses have quicker AI rollouts because of the pandemic.

More of the report shows that:

1 **Trustworthy and understandable AI is important to businesses.** Because data available shows that, of all the businesses that deployed AI in their operation, 91% agreed that AI's ability to explain how it arrived at a decision is important.

2. **Ability to access data from any place is vital for the increase in AI acceptance.** As expected, about 90% of IT professionals who also air their opinion agreed that the ability to run AI projects from any place the data resides is crucial to the technology's acceptance.

3. The need to preserve Natural language processing is a major area of focus in recent acceptance. As at least a half of all businesses today are now adopting applications powered by NLP, even as about 25% of those who are yet to, are already planning to begin the NLP technology within the next 12 months, `the report stated; with Customer service at the forefront of the NLP use case.

On the major barriers to AI acceptance, the survey listed three main hurdles that businesses face when accepting AI to include:

14. AI expertise or knowledge affecting 39%

15. Growing data complexity and data silos affecting 32%,

16. lack of requisite apparatuses/platforms for the development of AI models, affecting 28%.

To say the least, enterprises are still facing challenges in deploying AI. Even those organizations that have effectively deployed AI are still trying to understand how the use of AI can improve revenue rather than just using it. An idea that was chronicled by **LAWTON** in an in-depth analysis of what was described as "last-mile" delivery problems in AI businesses, noted that companies are finding it much harder to interlace AI machinery into existing business processes compared to building or buying AI models that will optimize those processes.

In his view, Ian Xiao, manager at Deloitte Omnia AI, projected that most companies will use between 10% and 40% of their spending on machine learning projects. I think he is right with this assertion.

The various challenges possibly hindering the effective integration of AI into business processes may be listed as follows:

Nonexistence of the last-mile infrastructure, e.g. integration platform as a service, robotic process automation, and low-code platforms required to link AI into the business;

Nonexistence of domain specialists who can evaluate what AI is good for; like thinking out which decision-making elements of a method is best automated by AI and how to reengineer the method.

Nonexistence of the right feedback on machine learning models, which requires a regular update to reflect new data.

Industry experts have all agreed that though AI deployment is emerging, the most important factor reported by almost all data scientists that have studied the processes was the need to work in synergy with the company's product experts. These experts with in-depth knowledge of their area of specialization, they stressed, will provide the context and nuance that deep learning tools will not be able to on their own.

I would emphatically say here that applying AI innovativeness requires a considerate method that will adequately define people, processes, and technology.

Possible Steps for proper implementation of AI in organizations

It's already a known fact that AI comes in many forms including machine learning, deep learning, and predictive analytics. Also, NLP, computer vision, and automation.

And so, it is pertinent to understand how it can be effectively implemented in a typical business environment. I have already mentioned the importance companies must place on people, processes, and technology while adopting AI in business.

This is so because like other developing technology, new ideas kept coming up and industry experts are still studying and changing the rules even as they have advised companies to be a little cautious in emphasizing AI use; instead many agreed on what was described as "an experimental mindset" which they said will yield a better result compared to the "big bang approach."

Perhaps they're suggesting that companies should start with a hypothesis, then the testing and laborious measurement of outcome. Some of the very useful steps will surface as follows:

1. Construct a data facility.
2. State your primary business motivators for AI.
3. Recognize areas of opportunity.
4. Appraise your core capabilities.
5. Recognize suitable applicants.
6. Start Experimental AI project.
7. Establish a reference point for better understanding.
8. Measure incrementally.
9. Start major AI capabilities to prime of life.
10. Improve on the AI models and processes regularly.

Trends in AI: Giant chips,

I have read a lot about the difficulties in ascertaining how much development is being done on artificial intelligence by merchants, governments, and related institutions, and the speed at which the field is changing.

Talking about **hardware**, startups are evolving fresh ways to organize memory, compute and network to be able to reshape the way prominent enterprises design and use the AI algorithms.

Just recently, a vendor was reported to have started testing a single chip, which is almost the size of an iPad, according to the information available. These **AI giant chips** are said to have the ability to move data around thousands of times faster than current AI chips.

It will interest you to also know that even recognized knowledge like the difference between the GPUs and CPUs in running AI workloads is presently not reliable according to leading AI researchers. A team at Rice University is said to be working on a fresh type of algorithm, referred to as **S**ub-**LI**near **D**eep learning **E**ngine (SLIDE), which is believed would make CPUs practical for more kinds of algorithms. Recall that CPUs, themselves are "commodity hardware" that is readily available and less expensive compared to GPUs.

Commenting on this recently, Anshumali Shrivastava, assistant professor in the department of computer science at Rice University noted "If we can design algorithms like SLIDE that can run AI directly on CPUs efficiently, that could be a game-changer,"

Software discoverers within academia and the various industries are working towards the limits of present applications of artificial intelligence, in an intense quest to come up with responsive machines that can act like human general intelligence. Even those who initially antagonized the AI are now making peace with an optimistic view of the future.

Neuro-symbolic AI

Symbolic AI: - this is a method that emphasizes high-level symbolic representations of difficulties, logic, and search. Those who are advancing the course of **symbolic** AI seem to be working with proponents of **data-intensive neural** networks, in other to come up with an AI that is good at taking the compositional and fundamental structures of symbolic AI, image recognition, and natural language processing ability that characterizes the deep neural networks.

This so-called *neuro-symbolic* style is expected to make machines meditate on what they see. Which will indeed represent a huge milestone in the evolution of AI.

Neuro-symbolic ideas appear to be among the most exciting areas in AI at the moment, if the opinion of **Brenden Lake**, the assistant professor of psychology and data science at New York University, is anything to go by.

It is highly encouraging to know that AI developments that were like a dream a few years back are becoming institutionalized by merchants, as they have quickly incorporated these advances into commercial products, and open-source platforms. Technology giants like Google and Facebook are typical pioneers in these areas.

Still talking about the trends that will shape the future AI, fresh concepts and improvements were outlined in the 2021 trends in AI.

These trends include the following:

AutoML. Otherwise known as automated machine learning is one of the technologies that will get better at labeling data and programmed tuning of neural net designs.

Multi-modal learning. AI is also expected to improve on supporting several modalities like text, vision, speech, and IoT sensor data within a single machine learning standard.

Tiny ML. This is another AI that is being talked about: a machine learning model that will run on hardware-constrained devices, like microcontrollers used in powering cars, refrigerators, and utility meters.

AI-enabled conceptual design. The future AI is being modeled to play a major role in creative designs like fashion, architecture, etc. recall that a fresh AI model like DALL·E, can generate abstract designs of something entirely fresh with a given description: "an armchair in the shape of an avocado." is a good example here.

Quantum ML. This may not be obtainable at the moment, but the concept is getting more real as Microsoft and IBM, including Amazon, is making quantum computing resources and simulators available through the cloud.

The future of artificial intelligence and human intelligent

One thing that has characterized humans from time immemorial is their unique reliance on tools and the willpower to improve on these tools. The same is said of AI that started at some point. It held a lot of promises for improvement because of its inherent intelligence as a tool. Just like many who are hoping that the best of AI is yet to come, I am very optimistic that very soon it will take over almost every aspect of our human activities as a physical tool.

Very uniquely, AI-infused tools are significantly separate from other tools we have ever used in the past. Especially on the fact that they can respond to us when we talk to them, meaning that they understand us, and by extension have rapidly occupied our personal space by answering our questions and providing solutions to our problems. It is hoped that this synergy will improve further and arguably make the difference between human intelligence and artificial ones similar.

When this happens, related technology, which incidentally is rooted in or is enhanced by AI will also try to act like humans.

AI-powered devices like the brain-machine interfaces that will replace the need for verbal communication and related human attributes will come in handy here. This robotics that will make machines completely perform human action, including having a deeper understanding of the basic human intelligence is what the future holds.

You may have seen AI diagrams that look like the human brain, this, experts believe is the new approach towards unraveling the future technology that will enhance machine intelligence and make intelligence **bidirectional**: our machines and us will exhibit more intelligence.

5

DEEP LEARNING

D eep learning is an artificial intelligence function that acts like the human brain in processing data and producing styles for decision-making. Deep learning is an aspect of machine learning in artificial intelligence that has networks that can learn unsupervised from unstructured or unnamed information. Also called deep neural learning, deep neural network as the case may be.

To help you understand this better I think Deep learning is an AI function that imitates the workings of the human brain in analyzing data for use in recognized objects, speech, changing languages, and making decisions.

Deep learning AI can learn without human support, drawing from data that is both unstructured and unnamed.

For emphasis, Deep learning is a part of machine learning that could be adopted to assist detect scams or money laundering, among other functions.

Deep Learning functionality

Deep learning evolved alongside the digital era, which has brought about an increase of data in all forms and from every part of the world. This data, known as big data, is drawn from sources such as social media, internet search engines, e-commerce platforms, online cinemas, and so on. This huge amount of data is readily accessible and could be shared via fintech applications in forms like cloud computing.

Again, the data, which usually is unstructured, is so big that it could take decades for humans to understand it and extract relevant information. Companies realize the incredible ability that can result from unraveling this wealth of information and are rapidly adapting to AI systems for automated help.

Deep learning has indeed revealed huge amounts of unstructured data that would normally take humans decades to understand and process.

Deep and Machine Learning

I recently learned that one of the most common AI techniques adopted in processing huge data is machine learning, a self-modified algorithm that produces increasingly better analysis and patterns with previous knowledge or with fresh data.

If a digital payments company wanted to find out the occurrence or potential for fraud in its system, it could adopt machine learning tools for this purpose. The computational algorithm added to a computer model will process all transactions happening on the electronic platform; it also finds patterns in the data set, and identify any anomaly detected by the system.

Deep learning, a subset of machine learning, adopts a hierarchical level of artificial neural networks to execute the process of machine learning. The artificial neural networks are grown like the human brain, with neuron nodes joined together like a web. While traditional programs build analysis with information in a linear way, the hierarchical approach of deep learning systems allows machines to analyze data with nonlinear methods.

Electronics maker Panasonic is said to be working with universities, and research centers, and likes to develop deep learning technologies related to computer vision.

Practical Examples of Artificial Intelligence Shaking Up Business

I will try to examine some Ai machine technologies that are hell-bent on conquering the human race with constantly improving patterns of doing things like a man. While the sentient artificial intelligence machines are yet to come, these technologies are already in place and are seriously competing with humans.

In my quest to know more about the impact of these technologies at the moment, I took a closer look at a recent survey that suggests that more than 72% of Americans are worried about a future that will have machines do many human jobs.

More recently also, Elon Musk, the tech billionaire who has always wanted artificial intelligence regulated, was reported to have said that: "AI is more dangerous than nukes."

These Artificial Intelligence machines interestingly include:

1. Manufacturing robots
2. Self-driving cars
3. Proactive healthcare management
4. Disease mapping
5. Smart assistants

6. Automated financial investing
7. Virtual travel booking agent
8. Social media monitoring
9. Inter-team chat tool
10. Conversational marketing bot
11. Natural Language Processing (NLP) tools

When you understand the critical role the above AI technologies are already playing you will realize just how influential and intimidating it is to humans.

AI has made things very easy, I can't stop thinking how simple it is when one is making a Google search or requesting a product recommendation from Amazon, or even booking a trip online.

Robotics

While Industry leaders are yet to arrive at a consensus on what constitutes the term "robot". Roboticists likened robots to all kinds of programmable machines that can perform tasks. The definition is still limited to some extent because of the broad nature of robots.

Present-day machines referred to as AI-powered robots are said to have limited capacity in natural intelligence: capable of providing a solution to a problem in a limited capacity. You may have heard how

Ai machines are used in teaching Japanese students the English language for instance. This is just to mention as the list is endless. Let's examine the following

iRobot

The common Roomba iRobot is a smart home robot that can detect the size of a room and identify obstacles, remember the best routes for floor cleaning. It is also capable of determining the amount of vacuuming required about a room's size, without any human assistance.

Hanson Robotics

Hanson Robotics is AI building humanoid robots for the moneymaking and consumer markets that can proficiently talk with natural language and adopt facial expressions to send human-like reactions (Sophia). Interestingly, this robot is said to have accepted Saudi Arabia's citizenship.

Emotech

Emotech created Olly, a voice-controlled AI assistant that works like Amazon Alexa, but with a unique and evolving nature.

Olly's nature is a combination of machine learning algorithms designed to communicate to the robot to progressively act like its owner.

It can recognize an operator's facial expressions, vocal nuances, and vocal patterns to be able to start conversations and produce relevant suggestions.

Olly's pattern of response is peculiar compared to other voice assistants. I watched a YouTube video of how Olly can see a person resting in some way, interprets it, and understood that the person need rest. And therefore suggested some favorite music to help the person unwind.

AI Is Changing the Healthcare Industry

Those in the healthcare industry will attest to the usefulness of Artificial intelligence as a game-changer according to experts. Every aspect of the industry is positively affected. You can attest to the use of robot-assisted surgeries. There is also huge assistance in the area of data collection and processing, safeguarding private records, and so on.

The effect of Ai however on healthcare has been both positive-fast and easier diagnose, and somewhat negative-has skyrocketed medical costs. It is interesting how AI-enabled virtual assistants are helping to reduce needless hospital visits.

Apart from helping the nurses, workflow assistants are assisting the doctors in freeing up, up to 17% of their programs. It was also reported that pharmaceutical companies, with AI, are exploring lifesaving medicines that are quicker and faster in the health industry.

Let me talk about some amazing technology that will interest you:

Covera Health

Covera Health for instance is using what is referred to as "collaborative data sharing and applied clinical analysis" in reducing the rate of misdiagnosed patients worldwide.

The company's exclusive technology is using a structure that applied both advanced data science and artificial intelligence in sorting existing diagnostics, so to give practitioners accurate symptom data that is expected to impact the lives of patients

Well

Well is designed to give people a better life through easy access to medical guidance that helps in making informed decisions about the care they receive.

This exclusive AI-driven "health engine" personalizes health guidance to each operator and guides people in their health journey based on pre-existing circumstances and general health awareness:

- It uses a combination of personal and external health data in giving informed advice that is founded on other user experiences,
- provide analysis that can be redeemed at stores towards accomplishing challenges and backing up communities,
- help users with everything from screenings and questionnaires through prescription vaccination advice,
- recommend doctor's visits,
- Specific condition guidance, among others.

Path AI

This Boston-based Health Diagnostics, Machine Learning technology is designed to aid **diagnostic pathology** as improved technology for pathologists.

This algorithm is helping pathologists evaluate tissue samples and create more precise diagnoses. The purpose is to both improve diagnostic accuracy and also the treatment. PathAI's technology is capable of recognizing optimal clinical trial participants.

Having worked with the Bill & Melinda Gates Foundation and Philips, this high-volume prognostic test support tool was developed with a careful plan for viable access to its advanced diagnostic service area.

Pager

This is a practical healthcare management mobile app in New York City that applies artificial intelligence to help patients with negligible aches and related illnesses.

Her machine learning is used in analyzing clinical suggestions and data, to reveal cracks in a patient's healthcare management. It also makes healthcare endorsements. Apart from helping patients to plan appointments and make payments, the Pager app lets a user communicate with doctors and nurses through text or video chat at any time of the day, to discuss prescriptions and related issues.

Atomwise

This San Francisco-based deep machine learning AI is helping to rationalize drug discovery through convolutional neural network technology. Its algorithms are reported to be capable of retrieving "insights from millions of experimental affinity measures and thousands of protein structures to predict the binding of small molecules to proteins," according to an online report.

It is stated that it screens 10 to 20 million compounds daily and is well used in recognizing characteristics of patients for clinical trials.

Its unique ability to evaluate billions of compounds and categorize areas for drug discovery is believed to be a technology that helps chemists tremendously in their work based on its recent application in tackling Ebola and multiple sclerosis.

Massachusetts General Hospital

I still recall what I read recently about Massachusetts General Hospital partnering with NVIDIA to apply AI-powered machines in disease detection, diagnosis, and treatment processes.

With over 10 billion being trained in medical images in radiology and pathology, this program is rapidly facilitating testing and diagnostic know-how.

I heard of a recently concluded pilot program that used AI to prescreen patients with pneumothorax, often referred to as a collapsed lung, with promising results that have encouraged the plan to adopt it in the ER.

Self-Driving Cars

Self-driving or unmanned cars have come to stay, as someone once said: "What seems like the future, once considered science fiction, is upon us". The technology is gradually approaching that driverless reality that we all hoped for.

It's estimated that over 33 million independent vehicles will be available by 2040. All credit goes to AI that has fulfilled this futuristic technology.

What this means is that Artificial intelligence, rather than drivers will be driving our cars, as the newest cars now come with sensors that continually take note of all happenings in the car to apply AI in making intelligent decisions.

From the car speed, road conditions, pedestrian whereabouts, and related traffic issues, these sensors capture and apply AI in interpreting data and respond as fast as possible.

Below are a few companies that seem to be making the way for the autonomous driving prospect.

Motional:- Santa Monica, CA-based Autonomous driving and ridesharing that is applying advanced AI machine learning technology in making driverless vehicles safer and dependable; easily accessible too.

There is also **Cruise** which is doing wonders in data science with its cutting-edge autonomous vehicles that are among the first to enter our roads.

You may have also heard about **Waymo:** an autonomous fleet of vehicles in Mountain View, California, said to be Google's self-driving car project.

Luminar Technologies is LIDAR, Autonomous Vehicles in California. Luminar is creating one of the most advanced LIDAR-based vehicle vision commodities in the world. The company's sensors use fiber lasers that produce a self-driving car's AI system and an in-depth look at the world within them. The technology adopts artificial intelligence-based software systems to capture people, objects, events, road conditions, etc. from above 250 meters away, so an autonomous vehicle could have plenty of time to analyze and react to any given situation. I think this innovative technology has the potential to measure the speeds of different objects, so an AV can effortlessly decipher its most optimal move in a safe amount of time.

6

FINANCE

AI and the finance industry are a togetherness created in heaven some have suggested. The financial sector depends on accuracy, real-time reporting, and processing of high volumes of quantitative data to give decisions, all areas intelligent machines leverage in.

As the industry observes AI's efficiency and accuracy, it is speedily implementing automation, chatbots, adaptive intelligence, algorithmic selling, and machine learning into financial activities.

Recall that one of the biggest financial trends of 2018 is the robot advisor, an automated portfolio administrator.

These automated advisors adopt AI and algorithms to check data in the markets and predict the best stock or portfolio based on preferences. Wealth administration firms are turning towards Robo-advisors, not only because it is faster for both the organization and client time and money, but it also gives some extraordinary returns.

Here are a few instances of how artificial intelligence is changing the financial industry.

Betterment

Betterment is First Robo-advisor in Fintech and Impact Investing in NYC.

Betterment is an automated financial investing arena and a pioneer of Robo-advisor technology that applies AI to study an investor and build a personalized profile based on his or her financial plans.

Betterment's Robo-advisors adopt algorithms to automate tax loss acquiring, trading, transactions, and portfolio administration, all tasks that need a lot of human elbow grease and knowledge.

Betterment got $10 billion worth of assets under administration and as of the last two years was serving 250,000 customers.

AlphaSense

AlphaSense: an AI-powered financial search engine in NYC. AlphaSense created an AI-powered financial search engine to assist investment firms to get an informational edge.

Applying a combination of linguistic search and normal language processing, the program can process key data points across 35,000 financial institutions. The system's potential to scan millions of data points and get actionable reports according to pertinent financial data saves analysts many hours of work.

According to the company's website, over 800 financial firms use AlphaSense, including certain Fortune 500 corporations.

Numerai

Numerai: An AI-powered, crowdsourced hedge fund in San Francisco. This AI-powered hedge fund applies crowdsourced machine learning from thousands of data scientists across the globe.

The company brings out abstracted financial data to its community of data scientists, all of whom are applying different machine learning models to forecast the stock market.

The models are used against one another in a weekly tournament where developers compete for Numeraire (NMR), the company's cryptocurrency. The most accurate forecast makes it to the top of the leaderboard and is given more tokens.

But Numerai isn't about rewarding winners and losers. The game is simply a way to gather more models. The company's actual breakthrough is in how it synthesizes all of the changing approaches into a "Meta Model."

The diversity of the models around the "Meta Model" produces diversity in the portfolio, reducing risk and gathering higher returns. The more algorithms at work, the easier.

Industry impact on the company is top secret on the makeup of the fund, clients, and progress, but has over 35,000 data scientists contributing to its arena and has paid out some $15 million of its cryptocurrency.

Travel & Transportation

Artificial intelligence is gaining a mega-trend in the tourism and transportation industries. From making travel preparation to suggesting the most useful route home after job, AI is making it easier for us to move around.

Travel companies are particularly capitalizing on ubiquitous smartphone applications. Over 70% of users claim they schedule trips on their phones, assess travel tips, and research local landmarks, restaurants, etc. One out of three people noted that they've used a virtual travel assistant to plan their upcoming trips.

AI-powered chatbots are rapidly changing the travel industry by facilitating human-like interaction with customers for faster response times, better booking prices, and even travel recommendations.

For example, telling a travel chatbot you want to go to Paris might yield a natural language response suggesting flights, hotels and things to do in the City of Light based on a user's choices culled from the conversation.

I will talk about a few instances of how artificial intelligence is being used in the tourism and transportation industries:

Google Maps

These are Smart maps, it is useful in Search Engine, Artificial Intelligence, IT, and Video Streaming. Found in Mountain View, Calif. Google adopt AI in several areas, but the technology's particular application in Google Maps makes easier our commutes.

With AI-enabled mapping, the search giant's technology checks road information and adopts algorithms to determine the best route to follow, be it on foot or in a vehicle, bike, bus, or train.

In the future, Google plans to further grow artificial intelligence in the Maps app by using its voice assistant and creating assisted reality maps in real-time.

Aside from assisting millions of users to find their way every day, the popular ridesharing service Lyft, built its navigation features for drivers using Google Maps.

Hopper

An AI-Powered Travel Booking in Boston, Montreal. Hopper adopts AI to predict when you should be able to schedule the lowest prices for flights, hotels, cars, etc. The company's AI checks hundreds of bookings and will bring them out with the most up-to-date fees. I think there's so much more to this AI than I have mentioned here.

Applying historical flight and hotel information, Hopper will also make suggestions on whether the booking has reached its lowest fee point or if the user should hold out a bit longer for the fee to drop. To date, Hopper's AI-based algorithm has saved users more than $2.2 billion on flights alone.

Hipmunk

This Virtual travel assistant Mobile App, in San Francisco, provides booking fees for flights, hotels, excursions, and even vacation rentals using Airbnb. The company's "Hello Hipmunk," started in 2015, is an AI-powered tourism assistant.

By communicating with the bot on Facebook, Slack, or Skype, operators can book flights and discover vacation ideas around themes and interests. Travelers could also copy "Hello Hipmunk" on an email discussing possible travel plans and the bot will give travel suggestions. Again, the virtual assistant will check your calendar for upcoming events and start organizing a future journey.

"Hello Hipmunk" was one of the first-ever tourism chatbots and remains popular more than three years later it launched. Overall, the virtual assistant industry is growing fast and is predicted to reach above $15.8 billion in cumulative revenue by 2022.

Social Media

With over 2.77 billion active profiles on the platforms like Twitter, Facebook, and Snapchat, social media is trying to personalize and grow worthwhile experiences for users. Artificial intelligence might make or spoil the future of the industry.

With its potential to organize a massive quantity of data, recognize images, launch chatbots and predict culture change, AI is highly useful to an industry with billions of operators and about $45 billion in yearly revenue.

Again, advanced machine learning is likely to prove critical in areas that are under pressure to stop fake news, hate speech, and other wrong actors in real-time.

I will explain here another example of how some of the giant names in the game are adopting artificial intelligence:

Facebook

Image identification breakthroughs have helped a lot of users of Social Media. Found in Menlo Park, Calif, Facebook uses AI in Messenger chatbots, algorithmic newsfeeds, photo tagging proposals, or ad targeting, AI is strongly embedded in Facebook's platform.

The company's artificial intelligence team recently coached an image recognition model to 85% accuracy with billions of public Instagram pictures tagged with hashtags. The method is a huge breakthrough in computer vision modeling.

Facebook is also adopting a combination of artificial intelligence and human moderation to fight spam and abuse.

With breakthroughs in image identification and a doubling-down on AI research, Facebook is hoping for artificial intelligence to assist in policing the world's largest media platform.

Twitter

From San Francisco, this Social Media is using AI to facilitate the tweets you see on Twitter. The social media giant's algorithms want people to follow, tweets and news based on a user's individual preferences.

Additionally, Twitter adopts artificial intelligence to monitor and decides on video feeds based on the subject matter. The company's image scaling tool also adopts AI to determine how to crop images to focus on the most useful part.

Twitter's AI was recently put to service identifying hate speech and terroristic messages in tweets. By the first half of 2017, the company learned and restricted 300,000 terrorist-linked profiles, 95% of which were discovered by non-human, artificially intelligent machines.

Slack

Slack Software and Messaging, Collaboration Tool in San Francisco applies a data structure called the "work graph" to collect information on how the companies and their employees apply the tool and interact with each other.

Data from the "work graph" could then be used to train artificial intelligence models that will make Slack better. For instance, the company projects that the average user is bogged down by over 70 messages a day. Slack adopts machine learning and natural language processing in a way called "Highlights" to move relevant messages to the top.

Apart from "Highlights," Slack's search adopts artificial intelligence to assist users to pinpoint knowledge specialists and the channels where they could be contacted based on an analysis of who is speaking about what and where.

E-Commerce

I once scrolled through a website only to find an image of the exact shirt I was just looking at on another site. I need to thank artificial intelligence for that.

Implementing machine learning into e-commerce activities enables companies to grow personal relationships with clients. AI-driven algorithms personalize the user experience, improve sales and develop loyal and perfect relationships with customers.

Companies use artificial intelligence to use chatbots, forecast purchases and gather data to construct a more customer-centric e-commerce adventure.

Here's another useful analysis of how some prominent e-commerce leaders are implementing AI to boost sales and loyalty:

Amazon

AI-powered E-commerce Media in Seattle. Amazon is the leader in e-commerce AI. Whether it's the company's suggestions on which commodities to purchase, the warehouse robots that take, sort, and send products, or the web services that power the website itself, Amazon employs artificial intelligence in almost every step of its process.

In 2014 the company launched its AI-powered voice assistant, Alexa. Motivated by the computers on Star Trek, Alexa brought a wave of robust, conversation-driven virtual assistants. Amazon has rebuilt its business to suit artificial intelligence, with many AI projects. I once did a transaction on Amazon and was amazed by its algorithm.

Twiggle

An NLP for e-commerce search and Natural Language Processing in Tel-Aviv, Israel, Twiggle adopts natural language processing to grow search relevance and commodity awareness for businesses.

The joining of human-like deep learning and comprehension for the retail industry assists connect customers to what they need.

Twiggle has a site with two million visitors monthly and could lose as many as 266,600 customers from wrong searches. For those that use its search, the company recently made a 9%

increase in "add to cart" and a 12% growth in click-through rate.

Marketing

Marketers are allocating more of their budgets for artificial intelligence usage as machine learning has dozens of applications when it comes to successfully administering marketing campaigns.is this another reason for the budget rise? AI-powered tools have presently become widely available to small and mid-sized companies.

It is assisting marketers to build in-depth customer knowledge reports, processing pertinent content creation, and scheduling more impactful business meetings, regardless of large human influence.

Let's also examine a few instances of artificial intelligence in marketing:

Grammarly

San Francisco, CA-based Grammarly Software is like an editor reviewing your writing in real-time. Perhaps Grammarly can't do everything an editor can, it will assist make everyone's writing clearer and perfect. The AI-powered writing assistant joins data science, machine learning, authentication, and other forms of technology to make Grammarly as thorough as it can be when assisting professional writers and non-native English speakers. Grammarly is available as a stand-alone website and as an extension on email platforms, word processors, social media, and so on.

Amplero

This is an AI for Marketing, and Machine Learning, software for building customer relationships found in Seattle.

Amplero develops AI-powered marketing tools for a wide type of consumer-facing industries, involving finance, retail telecommunications, and gaming.

Amplero's algorithms discover patterns in data to develop dynamic audience profiles. Marketers can then adopt the company's software and machine learning power to run thousands of experiments.

In one case study, a company adopting Amplero to grow lowered its acquisition cost from $40 to $1 and showed an 88% lift in average revenue per postpaid client. Major brands like Sprint, Microsoft, and TaxAct adopt the company's AI tools.

Drift

Boston-based Drift adopts chatbots, machine learning, and natural language processing to assist businesses to schedule more meetings, assist customers with commodity questions and make sales more efficient.

The technology is particularly good at automating originally time-consuming marketing duties. For instance, once a customer is on a website applying Drift, a chatbot will pop up, request questions, and automatically put them into a campaign if they are a lead. Also, the company's "Drift Assistant" automates email responses, routing leads, and updating contact data.

Companies like Toast and Zenefits are adopting Drift to achieve quality sales leads in minutes instead of days. Drift is currently used by over 100,000 businesses.

7

WEAK AND STRONG AI

Weak AI

Weak artificial intelligence that is also known as narrow AI is a type of artificial intelligence that is limited to a particular or narrow function. Weak AI simulates human cognition. It can benefit society by automating time-consuming jobs and by analyzing data in ways that man sometimes couldn't. Weak AI contrasts with strong AI, a theoretical type of machine intelligence that is like human intelligence.

In summary

Weak artificial intelligence or narrow AI is a kind of artificial intelligence that is restricted to a specific or narrow task. Weak AI contrasts with strong AI.

Weak AI doesn't have human consciousness, although it may be able to simulate a few times. The best illustration of weak AI is John Searle's Chinese room thought analysis. This experiment opined that a person outside a room could have what appears to be a conversation in Chinese with someone inside a room who is instructed on how to answer conversations in Chinese. In this experiment, the person indoors would appear to speak Chinese. In reality, they couldn't speak or understand a word of Chinese absent the instructions they were being fed. That's because the person is better at following instructions, not at talking Chinese. They do not appear to have strong AI—machine intelligence similar to human intelligence—but they only have weak AI.

Narrow or weak AI systems don't have general intelligence; they have specific knowledge. An AI that is an expert at reporting to you how to drive from one place to another is incapable of challenging you to a game of chess. Similarly, a form of AI that can pretend to speak Chinese with you probably will not sweep your floors.

Weak AI assists turn big data into usable information by detecting patterns and making predictions. Examples of weak AI include Facebook's newsfeed, Amazon's referred purchases, and Apple's Siri, the iPhone technology that solves users' oral questions. Email spam filters are another instance of weak AI; a computer adopts an algorithm to learn which information is likely to be spam, then re-channel them from the inbox to the spam file.

Limitations

Apart from its limited capabilities, a few of the issues with weak AI include the potential to cause harm if a system malfunctions. For example, think of a driverless car that miscalculates the location of an oncoming vehicle and causes a deadly collision. The system also can cause harm if the system is used by someone who wants to cause harm; consider a terrorist who adopts a self-driving car to execute explosives in a crowded place.

A further worry related to weak AI is the loss of jobs occasioned by the automation of an increasing number of jobs. Will unemployment grow more, or will society come up with new ways for humans to be economically useful? Although the prospect of a huge percentage of workers losing their occupation may be terrifying, proponents of AI claim that it is also good to expect that should this occur, new jobs will emerge that we can't yet forecast as the use of AI becomes increasingly widespread.

Strong AI

Strong Artificial Intelligence (AI) is a theoretical type of machine intelligence that is equivalent to human intelligence. The main characteristics of Strong AI include the power to reason, solve puzzles, make decisions, plan, learn, and transfer information. It should also possess consciousness, be objective, self-aware, sentience, and sapience. Strong AI is also referred to as True Intelligence or Artificial General Intelligence (AGI).

In summary

Strong AI is that theoretical higher-level artificial intelligence that goes beyond Weak AI, or simulated human cognition, to involve problem-solving, learning, and improvement. Strong

AI increases the apprehension of people losing jobs to machines.

 Strong AI is a futuristic concept, not currently in existence. Some experts forecast it may be developed by 2030 or 2045. Conservatives on the other hand predict that it may be developed around the next century, or that the availability of Strong AI may not be possible.

Some theorists suggest that a machine with Strong AI should go through the same development process as a human, beginning with a childlike mind and increasing to an adult mind with learning. It should be able to associate with the world and learn from it while developing its common sense and speech method. Another argument is that no one will know when strong AI will come because there is still no agreement on what constitutes intelligence.

Weak AI merely simulates human cognition, but Strong AI could have real human cognition. With Strong AI, a single computer could theoretically work on diverse problems like humans could. This will mean that Weak AI replaces low- and medium-skilled workers, while Strong AI will hope to replace certain categories of highly skilled employees.

Risks and Rewards of a Strong AI
The possibility of Strong AI comes with big potential benefits and major concerns. Some people fear that Strong AI may become more intelligent than humans, a phenomenon referred to as singularity. The plan is that Strong AI will be so

intelligent that it can change itself and pursue a personal goal without human intervention, perhaps in ways that are harmful to humans. Killer robots like in the movie readily come to mind here. Is it possible to have a Strong AI programmed with desirable moral values? And what could those desirable values be like? Further research into these problems could help stop the possibility of robots that can turn against humanity.

Another big concern is that AI will increasingly move jobs away from people, resulting in unemployment – even for skill-intensive white-collar jobs, especially if Strong AI comes to play. However, just as the Industrial Revolution dramatically affected jobs, an AI Revolution could result not in massive unemployment, but a big employment change. Strong AI could have a significant impact on society with increase productivity and wealth. Humans could do jobs that we can't even imagine today. Another possibility is that the government will have to step in, to provide a safety net for those displaced by AI.

www.ingramcontent.com/pod-product-compliance
Lightning Source LLC
LaVergne TN
LVHW051613050326
832903LV00033B/4481